# GRATITUDE PLANNER

52 Week Daily Planner Filled

With Inspirational Quotes

This Planner belongs to:

_____

Copyright © 2020 Brenda Nathan

All rights reserved.

ISBN: 978-1-952358-19-7

The essence of all beautiful art, all great art, is gratitude.  ~*Friedrich Nietzsche*

**MONDAY**

**TUESDAY**

**WEDNESDAY**

**THURSDAY**

**FRIDAY**

○
○
○
○
○
○

**SATURDAY**

○
○
○
○
○
○

**SUNDAY**

○
○
○
○
○
○

**NOTES**

Write it on your heart that every day is the best day in the year.

*~Ralph Waldo Emerson*

**MONDAY**

**TUESDAY**

**WEDNESDAY**

**THURSDAY**

**FRIDAY**

**SATURDAY**

**SUNDAY**

**NOTES**

Life in abundance comes only through great love.

~*Elbert Hubbard*

**MONDAY**

**TUESDAY**

**WEDNESDAY**

**THURSDAY**

**FRIDAY**

**SATURDAY**

**SUNDAY**

**NOTES**

To forget oneself is to be happy.

~Robert Louis Stevenson

**MONDAY**

**TUESDAY**

**WEDNESDAY**

**THURSDAY**

# FRIDAY

# SATURDAY

# SUNDAY

# NOTES

Let the beauty of what you love be what you do.

*~Rumi*

**MONDAY**

**TUESDAY**

**WEDNESDAY**

**THURSDAY**

**FRIDAY**

**SATURDAY**

**SUNDAY**

**NOTES**

We never live; we are always in the expectation of living.

*~Voltaire*

**MONDAY**

**TUESDAY**

**WEDNESDAY**

**THURSDAY**

**FRIDAY**

**SATURDAY**

**SUNDAY**

**NOTES**

That which does not kill us makes us stronger.

~Friedrich Nietzsche

**MONDAY**

**TUESDAY**

**WEDNESDAY**

**THURSDAY**

**FRIDAY**

○
○
○
○
○
○

**SATURDAY**

○
○
○
○
○
○

**SUNDAY**

○
○
○
○
○
○

**NOTES**

The only true wisdom is in knowing you know nothing.

*~Socrates*

**MONDAY**

**TUESDAY**

**WEDNESDAY**

**THURSDAY**

**FRIDAY**

**SATURDAY**

**SUNDAY**

**NOTES**

It's not what happens to you, but how you react to it that matters.

*~Epictetus*

**MONDAY**

**TUESDAY**

**WEDNESDAY**

**THURSDAY**

**FRIDAY**

**SATURDAY**

**SUNDAY**

**NOTES**

This world is but a canvas to our imagination.

~*Henry David Thoreau*

**MONDAY**

**TUESDAY**

**WEDNESDAY**

**THURSDAY**

**FRIDAY**

**SATURDAY**

**SUNDAY**

**NOTES**

Never lose an opportunity of seeing anything beautiful, for beauty is God's handwriting.
~*Ralph Waldo Emerson*

**MONDAY**

**TUESDAY**

**WEDNESDAY**

**THURSDAY**

**FRIDAY**

**SATURDAY**

**SUNDAY**

**NOTES**

Adventure is not outside man; it is within.

~*George Eliot*

**MONDAY**

**TUESDAY**

**WEDNESDAY**

**THURSDAY**

**FRIDAY**

**SATURDAY**

**SUNDAY**

**NOTES**

Our greatest glory is not in never falling, but in rising every time we fall.
*~Confucius*

**MONDAY**

**TUESDAY**

**WEDNESDAY**

**THURSDAY**

**FRIDAY**

**SATURDAY**

**SUNDAY**

**NOTES**

Life is the flower for which love is the honey.

*~Victor Hugo*

**MONDAY**

**TUESDAY**

**WEDNESDAY**

**THURSDAY**

**FRIDAY** _____

_____     ○ _____
_____     ○ _____
_____     ○ _____
_____     ○ _____
_____     ○ _____
_____     ○ _____

**SATURDAY** _____

_____     ○ _____
_____     ○ _____
_____     ○ _____
_____     ○ _____
_____     ○ _____
_____     ○ _____

**SUNDAY** _____

_____     ○ _____
_____     ○ _____
_____     ○ _____
_____     ○ _____
_____     ○ _____
_____     ○ _____

**NOTES** _____

_____
_____

To live is so startling it leaves little time for anything else.

*~Emily Dickinson*

**MONDAY**

**TUESDAY**

**WEDNESDAY**

**THURSDAY**

**FRIDAY**

**SATURDAY**

**SUNDAY**

**NOTES**

To love oneself is the beginning of a lifelong romance.

*~Oscar Wilde*

**MONDAY**

**TUESDAY**

**WEDNESDAY**

**THURSDAY**

**FRIDAY**

**SATURDAY**

**SUNDAY**

**NOTES**

It's not what you look at that matters, it's what you see.

*~Henry David Thoreau*

**MONDAY**

**TUESDAY**

**WEDNESDAY**

**THURSDAY**

**FRIDAY**

**SATURDAY**

**SUNDAY**

**NOTES**

A single grateful thought toward heaven is the most perfect prayer.
~*Gotthold Ephraim Lessing*

## MONDAY

## TUESDAY

## WEDNESDAY

## THURSDAY

**FRIDAY**

**SATURDAY**

**SUNDAY**

**NOTES**

The most wasted day of all is that on which we have not laughed.
~Nicolas Chamfort

**MONDAY**

**TUESDAY**

**WEDNESDAY**

**THURSDAY**

**FRIDAY**

**SATURDAY**

**SUNDAY**

**NOTES**

Appreciation is a wonderful thing: It makes what is excellent in others belong to us as well.

*~Voltaire*

**MONDAY**

**TUESDAY**

**WEDNESDAY**

**THURSDAY**

**FRIDAY**

**SATURDAY**

**SUNDAY**

**NOTES**

God has two dwellings; one in heaven, and the other in a meek and thankful heart.

*~Izaak Walton*

**MONDAY**

**TUESDAY**

**WEDNESDAY**

**THURSDAY**

**FRIDAY**

**SATURDAY**

**SUNDAY**

**NOTES**

Prayer should be the key of the day and the lock of the night.

*~George Herbert*

## MONDAY

## TUESDAY

## WEDNESDAY

## THURSDAY

**FRIDAY**

**SATURDAY**

**SUNDAY**

**NOTES**

The art of being happy lies in the power of extracting happiness from common things. *~Henry Ward Beecher*

**MONDAY**

**TUESDAY**

**WEDNESDAY**

**THURSDAY**

**FRIDAY**

**SATURDAY**

**SUNDAY**

**NOTES**

When unhappy, one doubts everything; when happy, one doubts nothing.
~Joseph Roux

**MONDAY**

**TUESDAY**

**WEDNESDAY**

**THURSDAY**

**FRIDAY**

**SATURDAY**

**SUNDAY**

**NOTES**

We have it in our power to begin the world over again.

*~Thomas Paine*

**MONDAY**

**TUESDAY**

**WEDNESDAY**

**THURSDAY**

**FRIDAY**

**SATURDAY**

**SUNDAY**

**NOTES**

To the mind that is still, the whole universe surrenders.

*~Lao Tzu*

**MONDAY**

**TUESDAY**

**WEDNESDAY**

**THURSDAY**

**FRIDAY**

**SATURDAY**

**SUNDAY**

**NOTES**

A loving heart is the beginning of all knowledge.

~*Thomas Carlyle*

**MONDAY**

**TUESDAY**

**WEDNESDAY**

**THURSDAY**

**FRIDAY**

**SATURDAY**

**SUNDAY**

**NOTES**

Our happiness depends on wisdom all the way.

*~Sophocles*

**MONDAY**

**TUESDAY**

**WEDNESDAY**

**THURSDAY**

**FRIDAY**

**SATURDAY**

**SUNDAY**

**NOTES**

Love is the joy of the good, the wonder of the wise, the amazement of the Gods.

*~Plato*

**MONDAY**

**TUESDAY**

**WEDNESDAY**

**THURSDAY**

**FRIDAY**

**SATURDAY**

**SUNDAY**

**NOTES**

The most certain sign of wisdom is cheerfulness.

~Michel de Montaigne

## MONDAY

## TUESDAY

## WEDNESDAY

## THURSDAY

**FRIDAY**

**SATURDAY**

**SUNDAY**

**NOTES**

The most certain sign of wisdom is cheerfulness.

*~Michel de Montaigne*

**MONDAY**

**TUESDAY**

**WEDNESDAY**

**THURSDAY**

## FRIDAY

- 
- 
- 
- 
- 
- 

## SATURDAY

- 
- 
- 
- 
- 
- 

## SUNDAY

- 
- 
- 
- 
- 
- 

## NOTES

From a small seed a mighty trunk may grow.

*~Aeschylus*

**MONDAY**

**TUESDAY**

**WEDNESDAY**

**THURSDAY**

**FRIDAY**

**SATURDAY**

**SUNDAY**

**NOTES**

Happiness resides not in possessions, and not in gold, happiness dwells in the soul.
*~Democritus*

**MONDAY**

**TUESDAY**

**WEDNESDAY**

**THURSDAY**

**FRIDAY**

**SATURDAY**

**SUNDAY**

**NOTES**

Always laugh when you can. It is cheap medicine.

*~Lord Byron*

## MONDAY

## TUESDAY

## WEDNESDAY

## THURSDAY

**FRIDAY**

- 
- 
- 
- 
- 
- 

**SATURDAY**

- 
- 
- 
- 
- 
- 

**SUNDAY**

- 
- 
- 
- 
- 
- 

**NOTES**

Contentment consist not in adding more fuel, but in taking away some fire.
*~Thomas Fuller*

**MONDAY**

**TUESDAY**

**WEDNESDAY**

**THURSDAY**

**FRIDAY**

**SATURDAY**

**SUNDAY**

**NOTES**

Enthusiasm is the genius of sincerity and truth accomplishes no victories without it.  ~*Edward G. Bulwer-Lytton*

**MONDAY**

**TUESDAY**

**WEDNESDAY**

**THURSDAY**

**FRIDAY**

**SATURDAY**

**SUNDAY**

**NOTES**

Just as our eyes need light in order to see, our minds need ideas in order to conceive.   ~*Nicolas Malebranche*

**MONDAY**

**TUESDAY**

**WEDNESDAY**

**THURSDAY**

**FRIDAY**

- 
- 
- 
- 
- 
- 

**SATURDAY**

- 
- 
- 
- 
- 
- 

**SUNDAY**

- 
- 
- 
- 
- 
- 

**NOTES**

No man's knowledge here can go beyond his experience.

*~John Locke*

**MONDAY**

**TUESDAY**

**WEDNESDAY**

**THURSDAY**

**FRIDAY**

**SATURDAY**

**SUNDAY**

**NOTES**

Our life is what our thoughts make it.

~Marcus Aurelius

**MONDAY**

**TUESDAY**

**WEDNESDAY**

**THURSDAY**

**FRIDAY**

**SATURDAY**

**SUNDAY**

**NOTES**

Beauty awakens the soul to act.

*~Dante Alighieri*

**MONDAY**

**TUESDAY**

**WEDNESDAY**

**THURSDAY**

**FRIDAY**

**SATURDAY**

**SUNDAY**

**NOTES**

Creativity is not the finding of a thing, but the making something out of it after it is found.  ~*James Russell Lowell*

**MONDAY**

**TUESDAY**

**WEDNESDAY**

**THURSDAY**

**FRIDAY**

**SATURDAY**

**SUNDAY**

**NOTES**

There is nothing on this earth more to be prized than true friendship.
*~Thomas Aquinas*

**MONDAY**

**TUESDAY**

**WEDNESDAY**

**THURSDAY**

**FRIDAY**

**SATURDAY**

**SUNDAY**

**NOTES**

That man is a success who has lived well, laughed often and loved much. ~*Robert Louis Stevenson*

## MONDAY

## TUESDAY

## WEDNESDAY

## THURSDAY

## FRIDAY

- 
- 
- 
- 
- 
- 

## SATURDAY

- 
- 
- 
- 
- 
- 

## SUNDAY

- 
- 
- 
- 
- 
- 

## NOTES

Man's greatness lies in his power of thought.

*~Blaise Pascal*

**MONDAY**

**TUESDAY**

**WEDNESDAY**

**THURSDAY**

**FRIDAY**

**SATURDAY**

**SUNDAY**

**NOTES**

The mountains are calling and I must go.

*~John Muir*

**MONDAY**

**TUESDAY**

**WEDNESDAY**

**THURSDAY**

**FRIDAY**

**SATURDAY**

**SUNDAY**

**NOTES**

I dwell in possibility.

~Emily Dickinson

**MONDAY**

**TUESDAY**

**WEDNESDAY**

**THURSDAY**

**FRIDAY**

**SATURDAY**

**SUNDAY**

**NOTES**

Good actions give strength to ourselves and inspire good actions in others.

~*Plato*

**MONDAY**

**TUESDAY**

**WEDNESDAY**

**THURSDAY**

**FRIDAY**

**SATURDAY**

**SUNDAY**

**NOTES**

Our best successes often come after our greatest disappointments.
~Henry Ward Beecher

**MONDAY**

**TUESDAY**

**WEDNESDAY**

**THURSDAY**

**FRIDAY**

**SATURDAY**

**SUNDAY**

**NOTES**

The way to know life is to love many things.

*~Vincent Van Gogh*

**MONDAY**

**TUESDAY**

**WEDNESDAY**

**THURSDAY**

**FRIDAY**

**SATURDAY**

**SUNDAY**

**NOTES**

Keep love in your heart. A life without it is like a sunless garden when the flowers are dead.
*~Oscar Wilde*

**MONDAY**

**TUESDAY**

**WEDNESDAY**

**THURSDAY**

**FRIDAY**

**SATURDAY**

**SUNDAY**

**NOTES**

The future is purchased by the present.

~*Samuel Johnson*

**MONDAY**

**TUESDAY**

**WEDNESDAY**

**THURSDAY**

**FRIDAY**

**SATURDAY**

**SUNDAY**

**NOTES**

Nothing is a waste of time if you use the experience wisely.

*~Auguste Rodin*

**MONDAY**

**TUESDAY**

**WEDNESDAY**

**THURSDAY**

**FRIDAY**

- 
- 
- 
- 
- 
- 

**SATURDAY**

- 
- 
- 
- 
- 
- 

**SUNDAY**

- 
- 
- 
- 
- 
- 

**NOTES**

Remember when life's path is steep to keep your mind even.

*~Horace*

**MONDAY**

**TUESDAY**

**WEDNESDAY**

**THURSDAY**

**FRIDAY**

**SATURDAY**

**SUNDAY**

**NOTES**

Ask me not what I have, but what I am.

*~Heinrich Heine*

**MONDAY**

**TUESDAY**

**WEDNESDAY**

**THURSDAY**

**FRIDAY**

**SATURDAY**

**SUNDAY**

**NOTES**

The best preparation for tomorrow is to do today's work superbly well.
*~William Osler*

www.ingramcontent.com/pod-product-compliance
Lightning Source LLC
Chambersburg PA
CBHW060045230426
43661CB00004B/665